14 Messages of Hope

14 Messages of Hope

Thoughts for Funerals and Other Occasions

Friedrich Rest

PULPIT LIBRARY

BAKER BOOK HOUSE
Grand Rapids, Michigan 49506

To leaders of small and large groups who wish to underscore the foundations of Christian hope and to persons who wish to kindle their faith through reading, meditation, and prayer.

Contents

Preface

Some time ago an associate pastor came to me from a church of young families in a growing suburban area. During his two years with this church there were no deaths in the congregation and the demands for pastoral assistance were few. This young minister became aware of his need for more varied pastoral experience and wanted to learn and serve in a larger church. My church called him to serve with me, and for the first few months we had weekly pastoral sessions on one phase of the Christian ministry after another—weddings, baptisms, pastoral calls, counseling, and funerals. Some of the points we talked about regarding funerals were incorporated into "Guidelines for Planning Funerals," which eventually became the *Funeral Handbook*, published in 1982.

My friend was interested in people who were bereaved—what to say to them, how to comfort and challenge them. To make his funeral messages relevant, he learned to use an anecdote, a personal observation, a quotation given by the deceased one's family, a confirmation memory verse, a favorite passage of Scripture, an often-used motto, or other information.

A funeral message may thus be cast differently for different people, and the message may vary further in diverse circumstances. The deceased may be a child, a parent, a spouse, an aged person, a person who died in an accident, or one who committed suicide. Sometimes an aged Christian, a long-time member of the church, has died. At other times the deceased may be a friend or an acquaintance who knew little or nothing of the Christian faith, or one who once believed but drifted away from the Lord. Imaginative and creative adaptations of small but important points are often called for. The minister will frequently find himself facing people who need a review or fresh look at the value of Christian faith. Thus I have written this sermonic follow-up of my aforementioned work on funeral services.

To make this volume as practical as possible, I have included sermons I have preached with adaptations and changes at various funerals. Sometimes I found it necessary to develop a thought more completely than I have here and at other times I condensed my thoughts in order to stress a more vital point.

My hope is that this book will be received in the spirit I offer it: as a collection of thought-producing sermons for perusal and free adaptation.

1

A Garden of *P*'s
Expounding on Psalm 23

Text: *Read Psalm 23*

Readers of the Bible turn often to a book that many have used daily for more than two thousand years. This book of the Bible, which has helped to form the language of Christian worship with its aspirations, eternal hope, and deep trust, is, of course, the Book of Psalms. A guide for dealing with the affairs of everyday life, this book draws aside the curtain between ourselves and our mighty God and helps us to see Him as a compassionate, patient, supportive hearer of our problems and griefs.

Probably the best-known and most loved portion of this book is Psalm 23, a psalm that throbs with trust, humility, and hope as if it came from the heart of man and the throne of God. Someone summed up the idea like this: "It is a divinely simple psalm, and it is simply divine!" Psalm 23 says and implies so much that discipline will be needed to limit this meditation.

It is possible to think of this psalm as a garden—a garden of *P*'s—as a colleague of mine once called it. Perhaps he had thoughts grouped under words like possession, provision, position, pardon, progress, providence, protection, promise, and even Paradise!

Possession

"The LORD is my shepherd." Our parents or a Sunday school teacher may have taught us this verse with the assurance that God is truly our Shepherd. A good shepherd knows his sheep individually. We think of Jesus Christ as our Good Shepherd (John 10:11).

Provision

"I shall not want." God, who made the world and sends rain and sunshine on the just and unjust, is able to provide for the needs of sheep. Those of us who have traveled to the Holy Land will never forget the verdant pastures of Samaria in the springtime.

An expression many of us have heard tells us to "take time to smell the flowers." We need to be reminded to rejoice in the simple things of life—food and drink, air to breathe, ground to walk on, life within, and friends around us.

Position

"He maketh me lie down in green pastures." After the sheep have been satisfied in the pastures during the best grazing time, they are ready to lie down. Time for relaxation is a time when we may gain a new perspective. People sometimes comment after a period of hospitalization that enforced idleness has given them an opportunity to think,

meditate, and pray in a different way. Even though they didn't want to be hospitalized, they feel it has been good for them. Unhurried moments of reflection may be among the most valuable times of our lives, whether these moments come to us when we are healthy or when we are ill.

Pardon

"He leadeth me beside still waters. He restoreth my soul." Whenever the shepherd provides water for the sheep, it is refreshing, whether it is given in early spring or in the dry months between April and November in Palestine.

The refreshment we speak of most often in the Christian life comes to us in terms of forgiveness and hope. Sometimes in the church—with its altar, pulpit, stained-glass windows, organ music, and hymns—we feel refreshed, renewed. We might feel like singing Gerhard Tersteegen's hymn more fervently than ever:

> I sing the praise of love unbounded,
> Which God in Christ has shown to man;
> I sing of love that hath been founded
> Ere yet the stars their courses ran;
> The love that offers free salvation
> To sinful men of every nation.

Or, when outdoors, we may say with Saint Francis of Assisi:

> All creatures of our God and King,
> Lift up your voice and with us sing,
> Alleluia, Alleluia!
> Thou burning sun with golden beam,

Thou silver moon with softer gleam,
O praise him, O praise him,
Alleluia, Alleluia, Alleluia!

Our need for refreshment stemming from the pressures of everyday living with its frantic pace, competition, defeats, and triumphs, is met through prayer, praise, fellowship, and meditation.

Progress

"He leadeth me in the paths of righteousness for his name's sake." Our faith is not just a private, personal affair. It has its social responsibilities. Critical times call for wisdom. We need guidance for seeking righteousness, fair play, and justice. Too many people are not treated fairly when it comes to distribution of this world's earthly goods. Too many others who are capable aren't doing their part.

Providence

"Yea, though I walk through the valley of the shadow of death, I will fear no evil: for thou art with me; for thy rod and thy staff they comfort me." The psalmist David, a former shepherd, was aware of the ravines, beasts, and robbers that threatened the sheep, as well as the green pastures and still waters that nourished them. The sheep are guided and defended as they walk through unknown and dark valleys. The courageous shepherd may face opposition, and the sheep may face physical hardship, but they do not fear. The friendship of Jesus, our Good Shepherd, is meaningful to the downhearted, the discouraged, the

handicapped. He is out in front of us, wherever we are led. Our Shepherd protects His sheep!

Protection

"Thou preparest a table before me in the presence of my enemies." The thought of protection is continued as we think of a shepherd inspecting the ground for poisonous plants or dangerous snakes. The early church placed this psalm in the context of Holy Communion, emphasizing that the Shepherd feeds the sheep as His main task. Spiritual food is to the soul what physical food is to the body.

"Thou anointest my head with oil; my cup runneth over." Olive oil, the cure-all in Biblical times, was provided for injuries. The Good Shepherd takes care of His people, whether the injuries be caused by sin, the common care and perplexities of life, or the grief at the loss of a loved one. Sorrows may abound, but we have a Savior who consoles us and invites us to come to Him for rest and inner strength.

Promise and Paradise

"Surely goodness and mercy shall follow me all the days of my life: and I will dwell in the house of the LORD for ever." At the end of this lyrical poem we find the sheep secure in the fold. The word "house" in Hebrew indicates a home with many familiar voices, a family with wholesome relationships. Eternity, with its joys and fellowships, is intimated here, as it is in the words of Jesus: "In my Father's house are many rooms; if it were not so, would I have told you that I go to prepare a place for you?" (John 14:2).

The Good Shepherd was willing to give His life for us

that we might live in His "Father's house." He died on the cross for us all, indicating the greatest love in the world. "I am the resurrection and the life. . . . whosoever liveth and believeth in me shall never die" (John 11:25–26).

God, then, is our Friend, our Guide, our Shepherd. He is with us to help, heal, support, and encourage us to trust and not be afraid, to walk and not be weary!

2

Seven Pictures and a Thousand Words
An Overview of the Christian Faith

For many years I have heard the famous statement, "A picture is worth a thousand words." Yes, a good picture can substitute for thousands of words and last for many generations without losing its message or appeal. Let's think of seven pictures that speak for a lifetime to the Christian.

A Scenic, Breath-Taking View

Imagine the sun rising brilliantly over snow-capped mountains, indicating the beginning of a new day and reminding us of God's creation of the world.

Moses and the Ten Commandments

Picture Moses coming down from Mount Sinai, carrying two tablets, his face shining with the inspiration he received from communing with God. This is another great picture with a lasting message for civilizations past, present, and future.

The Infant Jesus

Think of the Incarnation, the birth of Christ, and all that He means for the world. Picture the infant with all His potential for growth in knowledge and grace; Mary His mother, pondering God's gracious gift to her; and Joseph, standing by them in the humble stable.

Jesus Preaching and Teaching

See Jesus with outstretched arms, preaching the Gospel of God on a green hillside, with His disciples and many others listening.

Jesus in Gethsemane

One of the most reproduced pictures in the world is that of Heinrich Hoffman's Jesus in Gethsemane. Gethsemane is the scene where the Crucifixion event was wrestled with and agreed upon, and where Christians are reminded of man's will and the will of God. "Not my will, but Thine be done" is a perennial prayer of a multitude of sincere believers down through the ages.

Mary, Martha, and Jesus

We think also of the dual needs of listening to Jesus' teachings and doing deeds of service, remembering that this was the issue in the story of Mary and Martha. Martha was anxious about many things, and Mary had chosen the better part, yet both had valuable qualities.

A Bird Above Troubled Waters

A lasting picture that we could well keep in mind, were we limited to seven, would be that of a bird safely sitting in a tree over a raging river, churning with fierce rapids rushing over jutting rocks. Such a picture represents to me the statement Jesus made: "In the world ye shall have tribulation: but be of good cheer; I have overcome the world" (John 16:33). Tribulation, troubles, anxieties, set-backs—yes, all these and more await us. But, don't forget, victory is ahead!

These pictures in your mind more than convey my explanations of these words for all time!

3

In the Midst of Life
At the Burial of One Who Died Suddenly

Text: *"Though our outward man perish, yet the inward man is renewed day by day"* (2 Cor. 4:16).

T hose of you who have attended a number of funerals or memorial services may recall the phrase, "In the midst of life we are in death." You may even have wondered if this thought comes from the Scriptures, since it is so close to what a number of Scripture passages express.

Somewhere I read that this sentence originated with a monk in the Middle Ages, after he saw some men working high above a deep ravine. They were building a bridge and the weather at times was adverse. If one slipped or lost his grip, the fall would result in certain death. "In the midst of life we are in death," thought the monk.

The "Big" Death and the "Little" Death

Stanley Keleman has written a fascinating book entitled *Living Your Dying*. The book is not primarily about death, but about dying. Keleman, a practicing therapist, seminar conductor, and worldwide lecturer, talks in his book about dying on two levels, the "big" dying and the "little" dying. He states that we are "always losing and finding things, always breaking with the old and establishing the new." That is little dying.

In the Psalms we read:

> LORD, make me to know mine end, and the measure of my days, what it is; that I may know how frail I am! Behold, thou hast made my days as an handbreadth; and my age is as nothing before thee: Verily every man at his best state is altogether vanity (Ps. 39:4–5).

The basic truth of this thought is brought out in other psalms as well: "As for man, his days are as grass; as a flower of the field so he flourisheth. For the wind passeth over it, and it is gone, and the place thereof shall know it no more" (Ps. 103:15–16).

We Face Ultimate Issues

How much better it is to face ultimate issues than to deny them as so many in the world are trying to do. I sense a great fear of death, an approach to life as though it has no end, and an inability to accept ourselves as finite beings, unable to recognize that we are people who are certain to die in a matter of time.

Perhaps this temporary denial of death is good, in that we seek means by which to prolong life. I refer here to advances in medical science and hospital skills in particular Also, hope is good, and the will to live is good. The ever-present hope that we shall be spared a while tends to pro-long life and helps bring things into a truer perspective.

Other Helpers Will Fail

But there comes a time when it becomes obvious that we are decaying outwardly. We become weaker. We discover that the best others can do for us is to numb our pain and anxieties.

Gradually the truth begins to dawn, if we have the benefit of a Christian faith, that we cannot rely any more on the limited skills of people around us but must look instead for assistance from above. As Henry F. Lyte put it:

> Abide with me; fast fall the eventide;
> The darkness deepens, Lord with me abide;
> When other helpers fail, and comforts flee,
> Help of the helpless, O abide with me.

Our Inner Nature Is Renewed

When this truth grows within us, we begin to realize that it is not only true that "In the midst of life we are in death," but it is also true that in the midst of death we are in life! "Though our outward man perish, yet the inward man is renewed day by day" (2 Cor. 4:16).

New life springs within. We may be weaker in body, but we become stronger in spirit. We are beginning to experience the "little life" in a way that will help us to experience the "big life" that is yet to come!

Didn't our Lord tell us, "In my Father's house are many mansions; if it were not so, I would have told you. I go to prepare a place for you" (John 14:2)? We have this assurance from One who knew more about life and death, dying and living, than everyone else who ever lived on the face of this earth.

This is the life which the apostle Paul experienced even when he was in prison. "Be careful for nothing but in every thing by prayer and supplication with thanksgiving let your requests be made known unto God. And the peace of God, which passeth all understanding, shall keep your hearts and your minds through Christ Jesus" (Phil. 4:6–7).

4

As a Shock of Grain
For an Aged or Prominent Person

Text: *"Thou shalt come to thy grave in a full age, like as a shock of corn cometh [up to the threshing floor] in his season"* (Job 5:26).

Ripened Grain Is Like a Productive Person

For Job, ripened grain served as an analogy for a person's reaching his or her full age, "as a shock of grain [coming] up to the threshing floor in its season."

A great deal of activity preceded the arrival of that shock of grain at the threshing floor: the ground was prepared; the seed was planted; perhaps protective measures against disease and insects were taken; air, sunshine, and rain were needed, as was endurance through dry periods, storms, and cold spells. God deals with His children in a similar fashion, for we experience various difficulties and troubles while developing the talents with which we achieve our goals.

The departed person has reached some of the goals toward which he was striving. (Here successes and service may be mentioned if appropriate.)

23

Worthy Goals in Life

The harvest scene does not speak of an untimely cutting down of the grain; rather, it is "in its season." Worthy goals in life may be to live fully and die confidently. *To live fully* would involve growing physically until maturity, growing intellectually long after the challenges of formal education have ended, and growing spiritually to become more and more like Jesus Christ.

To die confidently means that we have chosen a mature Christian attitude toward death and the life beyond. There are some who try to deny the existence of death. To some extent we all avoid death as long as we can. Later we may learn to resign ourselves to it as an important part of the pattern of existence. Trappist monks, in their vow of silence, may say only the words, "Remember the day of your death," as they greet each other, but we can and should be able to put the thought into a more comprehensive perspective. We remember death but are not consumed by its reality.

Personally we may welcome death, for heaven is beautiful. Also, death provides a release from pain and from the weeds and thorns of this life; it provides a triumph over sin, grief, and loss, even though there may be a real regret because of certain responsibilities and fellowship we would still like to shoulder and embrace.

To Live Is Christ

A very wise person once wrote a letter from prison. He was an outstanding man, upright, exceptionally talented and energetic. In his letter he said, "For to me to live is

Christ, and to die is gain. If it is to be life in the flesh, that means fruitful labor for me. Yet which I shall choose I cannot tell. I am hard pressed between the two. My desire is to depart and be with Christ, for that is far better. But to remain in the flesh is more necessary on your account" (Phil. 1:21–24). The man, of course, was the apostle Paul.

Seven Deadly (Modern) Sins

Someone has said the seven deadly *modern* sins are: worship without sacrifice, politics without principle, wealth without work, pleasure without conscience, knowledge without character, business without morality, and science without humanity.

It is good if we are aware that God's manifestations are all around us. Sometimes people say that their busy life is too full for Christianity. "Worship is not my bag" an individual once told me.

If we have no time for God, maybe we are giving our highest devotion to wealth, pleasure, prestige, knowledge, business, or science. If I don't have enough time to get fuel for my car, air for my lungs, food for my stomach, inspiration for my life, or fellowship for my social inclinations, then perhaps my life is not developing in a normal, balanced way.

Summary

To sum up, we know that in life we have certain responsibilities. God's help is essential. "We plow the fields, and scatter the good seed on the land, but it is fed and watered by God's almighty hand."

Is it not mature to look at things as Mathias Claudius did?

We thank Thee, then O Father,
   For all things bright and good,
The seed-time and the harvest,
   Our life, our health, our food.

Accept the fruits we offer for all thy love imparts,
And that which thou desirest,
   Our humble, thankful hearts.
All good gifts around us are sent from heaven above;
Then thank the Lord, O thank the Lord for all his love.

We acknowledge that an aged person has been removed from our midst. We know also that this life was truly fruitful. Our gratitude is deep, despite the inward pain.

5

What God Has Promised
At the Burial of One
Who Suffered Long

Text: *"Come unto me, all ye that labour and are heavy laden, and I will give you rest. Take my yoke upon you, and learn of me; for I am meek and lowly in heart, and ye shall find rest unto your souls. For my yoke is easy, and my burden is light"* (Matt. 11:28–30).

Why Do We Suffer?

While the question of why there is suffering is a universal one, no one has ever found a completely satisfying answer. The problem has plagued people for ages despite persistent probing into the mystery.

Jesus had outstanding success as a teacher and healer. People thronged to Him to hear and to be healed. But then even Jesus suffered. Difficulties and problems arose, resulting in growing opposition, great pain, and death, before His glorious resurrection.

In Matthew 11 Jesus, aware of criticism, disappointment, doubts, and apathy, was still confident and continued the work He was sent to do for the salvation of the world. He looked around and invitingly said, "Come to me, all who labor and are heavy laden, and I will give you rest. . . . my burden is light" (vv. 28–30). What we see here is not mainly a system of thought, a philosophy or theology (although His total thought can be organized in a marvelous pattern), but a direction. The direction was to look to Him. "Come to me, . . . learn from me," Jesus said. The other writers of the Gospels help us to center the direction of our lives on Him who is the Bread of Life (John 6:35), the Light of the World (John 8:12), the Door (John 10:9), the Good Shepherd (John 10:11), the Way, the Truth, and the Life (John 14:6). What He said and did and what He is enables us to receive some of the most precious promises of God!

Be of Good Cheer

Jesus never closed His eyes to the problems of life. He stated with clear penetration, toward the close of His earthly ministry, "In the world ye shall have tribulation; but be of good cheer, I have overcome the world" (John 16:33). Spiritual blessings can come from suffering; joy can come to the sorrowful, for God's love is deep and they therefore are capable of feeling the joy of companionship as well as grief.

God Promises Strength and Rest

One of the ingredients we all need and which God has promised is strength. Even a great prophet like Jeremiah was deeply discouraged (Jeremiah 15), but he was promised victory and he could carry on. Those without hope have no strength or determination. Through the grace of God many people have learned to know personally what the ancient man of God meant when he said, "God is our refuge and strength, a very present help in trouble" (Ps. 46:1). A ninety-two-year-old lady, the last of her nine brothers and sisters, wrote a column for her nursing home paper, in which she said, "God will help us weather the storm."

Jesus has promised us rest if we come to Him. If we try to keep all problems and anxieties to ourselves with sheer will power, we are like machines without lubrication. We can't take our strength for granted. We may discover, for one reason or another, that our lip begins to tremble and our determination becomes weaker. We can't always count on our friends either, for sometimes they are busy and under great pressure. And we can't count on money because it takes more and more of it to do the same things it used to do.

At last we turn to walk humbly with God who can strengthen us to face life again. We discover that we need to keep thinking of the highest priorities, remembering what Micah the prophet said: "What doth the LORD require of thee but to do justly, and to love mercy, and to walk humbly with thy God?" (Mic. 6:8). To walk humbly with God may mean going on with many unanswered questions, but with an abiding trust in God's wisdom and will.

God's Grace Is Sufficient

Saint Paul learned that the grace of God was sufficient for him, after he had sought three times to have a thorn in the flesh removed (2 Cor. 12:9), for God's strength was made perfect in weakness. Even Jesus received a "no" answer to prayer when He asked in Gethsemane if the cup of suffering could pass from Him. Through prayer we sometimes gain an insight into what we really want and what God's will for us might be. We gain guidance also from God's Word. The psalmist wrote, "Thy word is a lamp unto my feet, and a light unto my path" (Ps. 119:105).

Sometimes people who have gone before us on similar paths help to lighten our load. A widow once said, "I get more inspiration from people who remember a trip or an incident or a word that my late husband said than from all the diplomatic silence by many, of never mentioning my husband's name in my presence."

Help may come, if we look for it. The psalmist found help when he looked to the hills. He said, "My help cometh from the LORD, who made heaven and earth" (Ps. 121:2). God cares for us and we need to look to the wisdom and guidance of God. There is help from above if we obey. God will help us adjust to life and even to be a blessing to others.

Jesus' Undying Love

Jesus' love for us was undying. On the night before His death He said to His disciples, "Let not your hearts be troubled; believe in God, believe also in me. In my Father's house are many rooms; if it were not so, would I have told you that I go to prepare a place for you?" (John 14:1–2). On the cross the following day He expressed undying love to the thief at His side when He said to him, "Today shalt thou be with me in Paradise" (Luke 23:43). And minutes later He said a word of trust about His own life: "Father, into thy hands I commend my spirit!" (Luke 23:46).

In Short, What Has God Promised?

Years ago there was a lady confined to a wheelchair, who thought about suffering, patience, God's promises, and how to cope with difficulties. Her name was Anne Johnston Flint and she wrote a thought-provoking, comforting poem entitled "What God Hath Promised."

> God hath not promised skies always blue,
> Flower-strewn pathways all our lives through.
> God hath not promised sun without rain,
> Joy without sorrow, peace without pain.
> But God hath promised strength for the day,
> Rest for the laborer, light on the way;
> Grace for the trial, help from above.
> Unfailing sympathy, undying love.

6

Will We Live Again?
To People Not Too Familiar with the Christian Hope

Generally the question, "If a person dies, will he live again?" is thought about most seriously at the time a loved one dies. Job asked it (14:14): "If a man die, shall he live again?"

An Important Question

How do you answer this immortal question? Your answer will determine to a large extent how you will act. Moreover, it will reveal how secure you are inwardly, whether you have any real comfort in life and death.

Before we silently formulate our own answer to this important question, let us ask, in imagination, a number of other people to see what they think. Through their answers we may be able to arrive at a thoughtful answer for ourselves.

A philosophical person says, "Generally speaking, we *hope* to live again." He goes on to tell about people in different countries and civilizations, with their customs, rituals, and beliefs, and concludes that we hope to live again.

We ask another. He is known as a very just individual.
He says, "We *ought* to live again. There are so many things
in the world that aren't right. There ought to be another
world in which injustices are made just."

Another person you go to may say, "I doubt it very
much. The grave is six feet long and about six feet deep.
That is about all there is to it, unless you can count a person
'living on' in his children."

An educator says, "I think death is like a school at gradu-
ation time. A good superintendent of schools would have
ways of continuing education after the elementary grades.
Death is like going through a door to a grade higher up in
another school."

"Death is a great adventure," says another. Sadhu Sun-
dar Singh, the late Indian Christian mystic, gives an un-
forgettable illustration. He compares man's life to the life of
an unborn baby chick. The chick doesn't believe until one
day it breaks through the eggshell and sees a vast new world
beyond the border of its former existence!

What Jesus Said

Despite the fact that many of these people have given a
lot of thought to this deep question, and some of them have
helped us to formulate some ideas, we stop to ask ourselves
if we have gone to the most helpful people in search of an
important answer. After all, when our car needs attention
we go to a good mechanic. When our watch needs attention
we don't just go to anyone and ask, "Can this be repaired?
Can it be made to run again?" We go to a watch repairman,
an authority.

A lady on a cold wintry day at a cemetery stopped me after a burial to ask, "Is there a life to come?" In the midst of the chilling wind I knew my answer should be short and convincing, so I said something like this, "The greatest authority we will ever know said, 'If it were not so, would I have told you that I go to prepare a place for you, I will come again and will take you to myself, that where I am you may be also.' That authority was Jesus Christ, speaking of the many rooms in his Father's house (John 14:1–3)."

She was listening intently, so I went on: "Think of other quotations from Jesus: 'I am the resurrection and the life: he that believeth in me, though he were dead, yet shall he live: and whosoever liveth and believeth in me shall never die' (John 11:25–26). 'Peace I leave with you, my peace I give unto you; not as the world giveth give I unto you. Let not your heart be troubled, neither let it be afraid' (John 14:27).

"Think of Jesus' deeds—wonderful deeds!" I said to her. "He raised Lazarus from the dead. He Himself arose from the dead. Doubting Thomas said, when he was asked to put his finger in Jesus' hands and his hands in Jesus' side, 'My Lord and my God!' (John 20:28)."

I went on: "There was something recognizable in Jesus, and yet after His resurrection some of His followers walked with Him quite a while on the way to Emmaus and didn't recognize Him until they saw Him break bread in a familiar manner. There is to be something identifiable about us in the resurrection and something mysterious. Saint Paul calls it a spiritual body, as opposed to a natural body."

The woman was very polite. I thought she was persistently interested, so I dared to summarize in different words: "Think of God's love for us. He sent His only Son, that whoever believes in Him should not perish but have everlasting life (John 3:16). What comfort in life and death we have in this solid reiteration of our faith."

We shall live again!

7

What the Future Has in Store
Around New Year's Day

Text: *"By faith Abraham, when he was called to go out into a place which he should after receive for an inheritance obeyed; and he went out, not knowing whither he went. By faith he sojourned in the land of promise, as in a strange country"* (Heb. 11:8–9).

The Book of Hebrews refers to the story of Abraham, Moses, and other leaders of Old Testament times who went on their way in faith, not knowing what the future had in store for them.

Abraham Looked for Stability

Abraham from Ur of the Chaldees did not know where he was going and what tests he would face and how his faith was to be perfected. He lived in tents, temporary places, but he looked for something more stable: "the city which hath foundations, whose builder and maker is God" (Heb. 11:10). He was promised a multitude of descendants, but the future looked drastically bleak at times, including the

37

many years when Sarah was barren. It especially seemed
that God's promise would remain unfulfilled when Abraham was asked to sacrifice his long-awaited son Isaac.

Moses in Unpredictable Times

The time of Moses likewise looked mighty uncertain,
from the days when he was put into a basket boat in the
Nile River to the days of wandering in preparation for
entrance into the Promised Land. He had to contend with
the slavery of his people in Egypt, a stubborn Pharaoh, and
finally an ungrateful, complaining people who were not
sure their daily manna and their life of wandering was
better than their life in slavery.

What Will the Future Bring?

We look toward the unfolding of the current year and
realize that we too do not know what the future may bring,
but we can have faith that God holds the future.

What were the characteristics of the faith that our Biblical heroes had? They believed that God exists, that He is the
mighty Creator of heaven and earth. They believed too that
He was interested in their welfare, their plight. Beyond that
they also believed that He would help them. Moses emphasized that they should believe in one God and have no other
gods before them, an emphasis that is still difficult to main-
tain when it is so easy to worship money, pleasure, government, science, or self! The Israelites continued to struggle
with the problem of the worship of only one God as we do
today!

The writer of the Book of Hebrews was enthusiastic in

his praise of the men of old who "received divine approval" because of their faith and their faithful deeds. He goes on to say, "Wherefore seeing we also are compassed about with so great a cloud of witnesses, let us lay aside every weight, and the sin which doth so easily beset us, and let us run with patience the race that is set before us, looking unto Jesus the author and finisher of our faith; who for the joy that was set before him endured the cross despising the shame, and is set down at the right hand of the throne of God" (Heb. 12:1–2).

When you think of Jesus do you have a certain picture in mind? Do you think of Jesus when He preached; when He prayed, as in Gethsemane; as he healed sick people; as He suffered on the cross; or in some other way?

Look to Jesus

The writer of the Letter to the Hebrews pictures Jesus as the pioneer and perfecter of our faith, enduring the cross, and seated at the right hand of the throne of God.

Lay aside the things that block your spiritual progress and look to Jesus. Introspection has its place and purpose, but receiving a vision of Christ and drawing inspiration and power from Him is something else!

8

The Prince of Peace
*At the Burial of One
Around Christmas Time*

Text: *"He came unto his own, and his own received
him not. But as many as received him, to them gave he
power to become the sons of God, even to them that
believe on his name: which were born, not of blood,
nor of the will of the flesh, nor of the will of man, but
of God. And the Word was made flesh and dwelt
among us, (and we beheld his glory, the glory as of the
only begotten of the Father), full of grace and truth"*
(John 1:11–14).

There were many gems that came from the
gifted pen of Isaac Watts. I want to call your special attention to a hymn, based on Psalm 98:

> Joy to the world! The Lord has come;
> Let earth receive her King.

What a great joy there is in the Christian's heart in this
period of Christmastide, to think of all the wonders and
benefits that have come to us because of the incarnation of
our Lord Jesus Christ. He has come to bring us more abun-
dant life. He has come to show us the way, the truth, and the

life. He has come to save us from our sins, to assure us of His presence. The salvation Jesus has brought is one of fellowship with Him, and He desires that we be like Him.

Jesus, in the words of our beautiful text, "became flesh and dwelt among us, full of grace and truth; we have beheld his glory, glory as of the only Son from the Father." (Here it might be appropriate to sketch the attributes of one who, like Christ, showed a willingness to help others. Say, "How much more we feel this is true of Christ, who personified God among people in Palestine."

This Is the Good News of God

Jesus saves us from despair and discouragement. The people of His day heard Him gladly because He spoke of their concerns and helped them where they were. He preached and healed people with various kinds of illnesses and handicaps. He had mastered life and was able to help others in their growing understanding and commitment. His uniqueness in part comes from the fact that His whole Gospel started not only from that little town of Bethlehem, but in the heart of the eternal God, who so loved the world that He gave His only Son, that whoever believes in Him should not perish but have eternal life (John 3:16). This is the good news of God: Jesus Christ, the Son of God and the Son of man, is the Lord of life!

The Time Was Ripe

Could Christ's life be fulfilled in our time as it was in His? He came to Palestine which was at the crossroads between Europe, Asia, and Africa. The Roman world had prepared the roads and government. The Greek world had spread a universal language. The Jewish world kept alive the hope of the Messiah as they were scattered throughout the vast Roman Empire. Jesus came into the world at God's appointed time.

Today is the day of salvation (2 Cor. 6:2). It is just the right time for us. We are aware of the transiency of life and we are ready to look beyond our own power to the world above.

9

The Cross and Human Need
During Lent or Around Easter

At least two distinctive hymns stand out during Holy Week.

A Palm Sunday hymn:

> All glory, laud, and honor,
> To Thee, Redeemer, King
> To whom the lips of children
> Made sweet hosannas ring!
>
> . . . .
>
> The people of the Hebrews
> With palms before Thee went;
> Our praise and prayer and anthems
> Before Thee we present.
>
> Theodulph of Orleans, c. 820
> *Tr.* John Mason Neale, 1854

On Good Friday, or whenever we think of the cross:

> O sacred Head, now wounded,
> With grief and shame weighed down,
> Now scornfully surrounded
> With thorns, Thine only crown;

45

O sacred Head, what glory,
What bliss till now was Thine!
Yet, though despised and gory,
I joy to call Thee mine!

Ascribed to Bernard of Clairvaux, 1091–1153
Tr. James W. Alexander, 1830

These hymns help to bring the triumph and agony of
Holy Week into perspective for us today.

What the Triumphal Entry Meant

Jesus referred three times to His rejection and death. He
was about to "suffer many things, and be rejected of the
elders, and of the chief priests, and scribes, and be killed,
and after three days rise again" (Mark 8:31). Similar statements made by Jesus on the way to Jerusalem before His
triumphal entry into the city, may be found in succeeding
chapters (Mark 9:30–31 and Mark 10:33).

The multitudes didn't understand Jesus on Palm Sunday,
despite these predictions. They thought of Him as a con-
queror that will destroy rather than the Messiah that will
save. They were still looking for force and military power.
Jesus wept because they didn't understand. He wept for
others, not for Himself, even when He was betrayed and
nailed to the cross.

The donkey was used to dramatize what wasn't apparent
to the disciples, despite repeated statements by our Lord the
Master Teacher. In ancient times the donkey was considered to be a noble beast and riding into the city was sym-
bolic of peace.

The Palm Sunday event showed Jesus personalizing the

expectations of the people, but with greater meaning than they understood. He was coming with something new and unexpected—the royal path of peace and love, and God's will transcending mere human anticipation. Their fondest hopes were not only fulfilled. They were to be transformed!

We should cast our garments of pride before Him because Jesus rode into Jerusalem to fulfill a task that gave us our salvation. Today, still, He wants to win the world through love and peace. We need to bow the knee and confess that He is Lord!

The Significance of the Central Cross

The ecumenical hymn, "O Sacred Head, Now Wounded," is a masterpiece of sacred music that expresses the sorrow of Jesus' suffering.

The hymn focuses on the central cross. It by-passes one cross, indicating the fearful end of the wicked. After all, many people have died on crosses, in gas chambers and hangman's nooses, so these kinds of crosses or executions are hardly worthy of the same kind of contemplation as focused on that central cross with its sacred head!

The other cross is touched upon as that malefactor raised a question to which Jesus brought an eternally significant saying, "Today you will be with me in Paradise." The hymn states it like this: "Look on me with Thy favor, Vouchsafe to me Thy grace." The central cross *gives* life to the righteous rather than *taking* life from sinners.

The Sacred Seven Sayings

"*Father, forgive them . . .*" This is the most inspired saying from the cross. Despite the nails driven through His hands and feet, the tearing of His flesh when His cross was dropped into the ground, Jesus was able to plead for the forgiveness of the weak and vacillating Pilate, spiteful Herod, blind Jewish leaders and dutiful soldiers. To me this is the most inspired saying of all that was said on Calvary because the natural reaction would have been hatred and vengeance.

Ed Markham, the poet, after a costly and disappointing business venture, wrote: "He drew a circle that shut me out—heretic, rebel, a thing to flout. Love and I had the wit to win. We drew a circle that took him in."

To day, shalt thou be with me in paradise" (Luke 23:43). This is the most significant saying because it indicates that Jesus will not be defeated by this earthly death.

The malefactor could have said, "I'm no worse than Caiaphas, no worse than Pilate or Herod." Instead he simply said, "Jesus, remember me when thou comest into thy kingdom" (Luke 23:42).

The only royal robe Jesus ever wore was the scarlet robe of mockery and insult; the only crown was one of suffering, the plaited thorns; yet the malefactor saw something kingly in Jesus.

The most understanding saying was: *"Woman, behold thy son!"* and *"Behold thy mother!"* (John 19:26, 27). They were to take care of each other when He was gone. The human element was kept in mind.

The most desperate saying was this: *"My God, my God, why hast thou forsaken me?"* (Mark 15:34). He was spit upon, rejected; He felt the full impact of sin. He bore the iniquities of sinners in His own person.

It would have been plausible to think God would take Him off the cross or comfort him; it would have been heroic for the disciples to have stood by, yet they fled; one would think the multitudes would have shown pity, but they mocked and jeered. Jesus was forsaken that we might not be forsaken. He died that we might live forever.

> Surely he hath borne our griefs, and carried our sorrows: yet we did esteem him stricken, smitten of God, and afflicted. But he was wounded for our transgressions, he was bruised for our iniquities: the chastisement of our peace was upon him; and with his stripes we are healed. All we like sheep have gone astray; we have turned every one to his own way; and the LORD hath laid on him the iniquity of us all (Isa. 53:4–6).

The most human of the seven sayings was this simple statement: *"I thirst"* (John 19:28). After about twenty hours of going without food or beverage or rest, with aching muscles, wounds in hands and feet, with parched lips and dry mouth, any human being would say, "I thirst." They put a sponge full of vinegar on hyssop and held it to His mouth. Our obligation is to help the needy!

The most purposeful saying was, *"It is finished"* (John 19:30). His work of redemption was completed. He was to reveal the reality and nature of God and to be obedient unto death. His prayer was fulfilled, "Not my will, but Thine be done!"

We, too, should follow the will of God. The way may be adverse at times, but following the divine way completes our purpose as God's children saved by Christ's sacrifice.

The most peaceful saying was His last: *"Father, into thy hands I commend my spirit"* (Luke 23:46). Someone has pointed out that every Hebrew mother was apt to teach this sentence to her child. Similar prayers are taught in different languages. The final word from the cross expresses faith and deep trust, and it is a good word for life as well as death!

Conclusions

The cross represents the worst affliction that man can bestow upon another and the finest thing that God has to offer! What could have been remembered as a Black Friday is now remembered as Good Friday. Instead of an emblem of suffering and shame, the cross is a symbol of God's love for sinful man! It has a glory of its own and can do wonders among people through the power of God!

The cross must be accepted! If the cross can accomplish all that, if Christianity can be that effective, why isn't it? Isn't this like asking, "If soap can do so much cleansing, why are there so many children needing to be washed?" It needs to be accepted and applied. The love of God is always here; God's love is everywhere, but it must be accepted in faith and applied before the real comfort and challenge of the Christian faith are experienced!

Look to the sacred head, to the cross of Calvary, if you want the inspirational power from the throne of God!

O gracious God, behold us as we in spirit gather around the cross and marvel at the mystery of your wonderful love. Empower the sacred seven words to become divine power and wisdom in our souls!

As on the cross He asked forgiveness for His enemies, we intercede for others, enemies as well as friends. In the name of the Lamb of God, who is taking away the sin of the world, have mercy upon us too, for our disloyalty, selfishness, apathy, and transgressions, and give us your peace! Implant in our hearts a spirit of mercy, gentleness, and patience, that we may love our enemies, rejoice in your love, and overcome evil with good.

Grant us a vision of your kingdom of grace and glory, whenever we repent and call upon you, as did the malefactor at Jesus' side.

As He died, Jesus united His mother with the beloved disciple. Unite us with our kindred in the bonds of love and peace. Help us to love the poor, protect the oppressed, and comfort the sad.

O God, forsake us not because of our guilt when our souls long for comfort. In loneliness make us aware of your presence; in unpopularity make us steadfast; in temptation send us your reassuring voice.

Refresh us with the water of life when our tongue is parched and our strength has failed. Grant that we may thirst for you and your righteousness.

Strengthen our faith in the redemptive work He finished. We thank you for the means of grace and the hope of glory. In the name of the great shepherd of the sheep, gather the sheep still outside the fold, that every knee may bow before you and every tongue confess that He is Lord.

Help us to trust in your all-sufficient sacrifice, that we may commend our spirit into your hands in deep trust. Keep us through faith and bring us to your everlasting kingdom and glory. Amen.

10

What Do You Accent in Life?
A Challenge for Youth

Text: *"Blessed are the poor in spirit: for theirs is the kingdom of heaven. Blessed are they that mourn: for they shall be comforted"* (Matt. 5:3–4).

The Common Accent in a Commercial Age

Sometimes when a person dies, someone asks, "What was he worth?" By this I think the person refers to material wealth, property, bank and savings accounts, stocks and bonds. The most common accent people put on life seems to be on material possessions. But Jesus said, "Take heed, and beware of all covetousness; for a man's life does not consist in the abundance of his possessions" (Luke 12:15).

A Fading Accent in a Sensual Age

A second accent in life is on our work. We ask, "What do you do?" "What's your line of work?" "Where are you employed?" "What kind of work do you want to take up when you finish school?" In this view a person is evaluated largely by his productivity. The person who works is the person who is very valuable to society.

The Best Accent

What is your main accent—acquiring goods? Working? A person can emphasize the drive for acquisition too much and become covetous, greedy, and morally insensitive. A person can become a "workaholic"—one who fills every flying minute with work and doesn't leave time for anything but sleeping and eating.

Jesus emphasized more than having ownership of things or productivity! He said, "Blessed are the meek"—the gentle, controlled people—"for they shall inherit the earth."

The Beatitudes of Jesus are thought of as "Be Attitudes." "The poor in spirit" are those who are rich in God's Spirit but poor in their own, and "those who mourn" may be trusting in God in such a way that their feeling of guilt is washed away in forgiveness. Their confidence in God's mercy and power helps them to understand that death is not the end, that God has great things prepared for those who love Him.

The accent is best placed when it emphasizes quality rather than quantity in life—the life of the spirit, the life within the heart and soul.

> *Our heavenly Father, by your love you have made us, and through your love you have kept us, and in your love you would make us perfect. We humbly confess that we have not loved you with all our heart and soul and mind and strength, and that we have not loved one another as Christ has loved us. Forgive us for what we have been; help us to amend what we are; and with your Holy Spirit direct what we shall become. Through Jesus Christ our Lord, amen.* *

*Adapted from the *Book of Common Worship*. For use in the Several Communions of the Church of Christ. ed. Wilbur Thirkfield and Oliver Huckel, E. P. Dutton & Company, 1932.

11

A Short Story
At the Burial of a Young Person

Text: *"We spend our years as a tale that is told"* (Ps. 90:9b).

It is possible to think of life as a long story, a short story, a love story, a story of struggles, a success story, a story of events in several locations, or a story of several stages in life. *(A sketch of the life of an individual may be appropriately told.)*

In thinking of life as a short story, we are almost forced to think of quality in life. Sometimes quality is more important than length. The prophet Micah tells us what God wants of us: "He hath shewed thee, O man, what is good; and what doth the Lord require of thee but to do justly, and to love mercy, and to walk humbly with thy God?" (Mic. 6:8). From this passage we would reaffirm our belief that religion is more important than ritual; it has to do with justice, fair dealings, kindness, sensitivity to the needs of others, and finding life by using our energies in kindly service—in short, walking humbly with God.

The life of _____ was short. David's statement, "There is but a step between me and death" (1 Sam. 20:3), is profoundly true. That step is a significant step, for it is serious and final. We do not know the time and place of our own death. No one can die for us, so it is a lonely step as well.

Each Person Is Precious

Each person is significant! The psalmist answered his own question like this: What is man that thou art mindful of him, and the son of man that thou visitest him? Yet thou hast made him little lower than the angels, and hast crowned him with glory and honour. Thou madest him to have dominion over the works of thy hands; thou hast put all things under his feet (Ps. 8:4–6).

The Heart Is Most Important

God looks on the heart. People look at outer appearances—clothes, sizes, shapes, and actions of other people. But God looks at purity, sincerity, and love within.

On the day of judgment this fact will be all-important, for God will judge each of us. Our outer appearance won't mean anything then. Only our heart will count.

Please God

To please good people is a noble ambition. To win the confidence and honor of those who are righteous, to speak some word, do some deed, exercise some virtue—these may be expressions of noble motives, restraining us from evil, encouraging us to heroic efforts, stimulating us to service.

More important than pleasing self or pleasing others is

pleasing God. It will help to remember that God is our Creator, Preserver, and Redeemer. It won't hurt to keep in mind that He is the One who gives eternal life.

We can please God by what we think and say, directing our lives to the highest goals God has in mind.

Trust God

We must learn to trust in God! The psalmist wrote:

To thee, O LORD, do I lift up my soul.
O my God, I trust in thee:
  let me not be ashamed,
  let not mine enemies triumph over me. . . .

Shew me thy ways, O LORD;
  teach me thy paths.
Lead me in thy truth, and teach me:
  for thou art the God of my salvation;
  for thee I wait all the day. . . .

Remember not the sins of my youth, nor my transgressions;
  according to thy mercy remember thou me,
  for thy goodness' sake, O LORD!

(Ps. 25:1–2, 4–5, 7)

12

Let the Word of Christ Dwell in You

An Overview for Mature People

Text: *"Let the word of Christ dwell in you richly, in all wisdom teaching and admonishing one another in psalms and hymns and spiritual songs singing with grace in your hearts to the Lord"* (Col. 3:16).

The apostle Paul wrote the words we have just read to the church at Colosse because he felt that his readers were about to emphasize teachings that were dangerous to the faith. A mixture of Greek and Oriental thought would crowd out the clear concept of Christianity. Therefore he wrote rather plainly.

A number of points could be underlined in the Epistle to the Colossians, but I would like for us to take to heart verse 16: "Let the word of Christ dwell in you richly. . . ." How full of meaning that is when we consider the teachings of Christ! Think briefly with me of what Jesus taught about God, the kingdom of God, righteousness, stewardship, and the rewards of the kingdom.

What Jesus Taught About God

Jesus saw God everywhere. God is interested in things we think are insignificant, such as birds that are fed, lilies that are clothed, and hairs that are numbered. He is a Shepherd who seeks the lost sheep. God is powerful and holy and loving, ready to bestow blessings even to people who are opposed to His rule and refuse His fellowship. In the Sermon on the Mount Jesus is recorded as having emphasized it this way: "I say unto you, Love your enemies, bless them that curse you . . . that ye may be the children of your Father which is in heaven; for he makes his sun rise on the evil and on the good, and sendeth rain on the just and on the unjust" (Matt. 5:44–45).

If God is like that, it would follow naturally that He forgives, like a father who sees his wayward son come back home. In the parable of the prodigal son the father was filled with compassion, running and embracing his wayward son and saying to his servants, "Bring forth the best robe, and put it on him; and put a ring on his hand, and shoes on his feet; and bring hither the fatted calf, and kill it; and let us eat and be merry; for this my son was dead, and is alive again; he was lost, and is found" (Luke 15:22–24).

But we dare not let our imagination remove the sternness of the risen Christ as it is pictured for us in a number of places, one of the most memorable being Matthew 25:31–33: "When the Son of man shall come in his glory, and all the holy angels with him, then shall he sit upon the throne of his glory. Before him shall be gathered all nations; and he shall separate them one from another as a shepherd divideth his sheep from the goats: and he shall set the sheep on his right hand, but the goats on the left."

When asked what was the primary thing God desires of people, Jesus said without hesitation, "The first . . . is, 'Hear, O Israel: The Lord our God is one Lord; and thou shalt love the Lord thy God with all thy heart, and with all thy soul, and with all thy mind, and with all thy strength . . . The second is . . . this, 'Thou shalt love thy neighbor as thyself. There is no other commandment greater than these" (Mark 12:29–31).

The Kingdom of God

Mark begins to describe Jesus' role in life by writing, "Jesus came into Galilee, preaching the gospel of the kingdom of God, and saying, 'The time is fulfilled, and the kingdom of God is at hand; repent ye, and believe the gospel'" (Mark 1:14–15).

Jesus spoke again and again about the nature of the kingdom, saying, "The kingdom of God is like. . . ," then going on by telling a parable. His truth was tangible as He taught people. He taught directly, illustratively, and authoritatively, and the multitude stayed long to listen. God is King, ruling in nature and in human nature, and His kingdom is one of the rule of God in the hearts and lives of people. People who listened to Jesus, steeped in the Old Testament as many of them were, knew that God claimed to be the authority in human life. They knew they needed to long for the kingdom and to trust God fully. Then as now, many people were not ready to let God rule, and they didn't understand what the coming of the kingdom meant. But it was something they could pray for, as Jesus taught them to pray in the Lord's Prayer.

Righteousness

Obedience to the law was considered the essence of right-eousness in Old Testament times, although some of the teachers of the Torah went deeper than this and talked of motives as well. When Jesus came He taught that rules and prescriptions are not enough. Inward goodness and right-eousness are needed. This inward life will result in deeds.

"Whoever would be great among you must be your ser-vant, and whoever would be first among you must be slave of all. For the Son of man also came not to be served but to serve, and to give his life as a ransom for many" (Mark 10:43–45). Thus obedience to the letter of the law is not enough.

Stewardship

People who have studied the life and teachings of Jesus have been impressed with the large percentage of Jesus' teachings that have to do with stewardship. The parables often deal with the subject. Remember the people with talents who managed the property with varying degrees of success while the boss was away, and the foolish virgins who were not prepared to light their lamps for the awaited bridegroom, and the son who squandered his money. God wants people to be responsible, good managers of time, talent, and treasure. In short, we should do our best with what we are and have. After all, we can't live without God for even a moment. We owe Him a responsible life.

Rewards of the Kingdom

"Let not your heart be troubled," said Jesus; "believe in God, believe also in me. In my Father's house are many mansions; if it were not so, I would have told you. I go to prepare a place for you. And if I go and prepare a place for you, I will come again and receive you unto myself; that where I am ye may be also" (John 14:1–3). Belief in the life to come is grounded in the character of a God who loves. Our hope is in Him. But the rewards of the kingdom are not confined to the afterlife. Loving, serving, helping—all these, if done in the right spirit, bring a kind of inner peace and satisfaction as well as good relationships with others. Communion or fellowship with God is the reward above all others, given to the pure in heart, to those who love God with all their being.

Let the Words Dwell in You

Much more could be said of the words of Christ. Let these and others dwell in you in all wisdom as you "teach and admonish one another. . . and as you sing psalms and hymns and spiritual songs with thankfulness in your hearts to God" (Col. 3:16).

13

Lead Me in the Way Everlasting
A Plea for Life Everlasting

Text: *Search me, O God, and know my heart!*
Try me and know my thoughts!
And see if there be any wicked way in me,
And lead me in the way everlasting!
(Ps. 139:23–24)

Our departed friend was a person who observed life rather closely. Our text turns observation of others and examination of things around to introspection and relates this to God: "Search me. . . . Try me. . . . And see. . . ."

Search Me and Know My Heart

We know that God is able to tell what is in us. No one can disguise faults or sins before God. Therefore if we want a thorough, reliable search, we turn to God, and say, "Search me, O God, and know my heart!"

Another way of saying this is, "Try me and know my thoughts!" Test me, give me a thorough analysis, to see what I'm thinking about, what I'm meditating on, what the condition of my inner life really is.

In a series of devotions a writer each day for a week shared some of her thoughts about gardening and the Christian life. She noticed the beauty and variety of weeds and asked her readers to consider and appreciate the shape, color, and smell of them, and to think how much God cares for all of His creation. When she moved on to consider the destructive nature of weeds, she compared them to human sin, taking her cue from Genesis where it is suggested that "thorns and thistles" came into the world because of sin (3:18). "Removing sin-weeds, like removing plant weeds, can be a nasty job. But it is a job that will pave the way for Christian maturity. What relationships or attitudes need weeding out of our lives?" she asked.*

I began to get more and more interested in each day's devotions because of her insight into the human condition through her work on weeds. If you let them grow, they begin to crowd grass or vegetables. Sins of human life begin to crowd out habits and tendencies we know are good. Weeds may be more deeply anchored at times than we suspect, causing us to rip up three feet of sod before they are out. In a similar manner, some sins may be rooted quite deeply in our past or our parents' or grandparents' past. "Hatred, blind nationalism, prejudice, and contempt for another class or denomination are passed from one generation to another. Somewhere along the way someone ought to be willing to name the sin and ask God to root it out!"

What intrigued me the most was the author's change in

---

*Patricia Honch Sprinkle, "Consider the Lilies," in *These Days*, vol. 8, no. 1 (January–February, 1978).

attitude about weeding. She used to say, "I'm off to weed the lawn," but later she learned to say, "Well, I'm going to weed a foot or two." Each individual weed needs to be pulled and a full afternoon will be needed to cover a part, perhaps a small part, of the lawn. She went on to say, "Perhaps the general confession of sins is a good thing for my whole life, but I need to ask God to forgive my sins one by one, like a cutting remark, a look of hatred, a feeling of envy, or rebellion against God."

The writer of the devotions began to think she was becoming an expert, so she volunteered to weed part of a friend's lawn. She discovered to her embarrassment that she yanked up a prized plant in her neighbor's yard that resembled a weed in her own. The lesson she derived from this is that it is best if we concentrate on our own sins and not worry too much about how to get rid of our neighbor's sins! Each person can work hard on his own life, in the light of God's searching and the insight of his conscience, and he may even be led to pray for another.

"Search me, O God, and know my heart! Try me and know my thoughts!"

Lead Me in the Way Everlasting

Consequently, we discover the seriousness of the last part of our text, "And see if there be any wicked way in me, And lead me in the way everlasting."

On our own we may never find the way, for there are many sins of thoughts, words, and deeds that distract us. When we overcome many of the sins that beset us we may discover that we develop a pride in our achievements. And pride is the sin against which Jesus spoke most sharply.

The Pharisees were people who had overcome a lot of sins. Many had learned to overcome selfishness enough to tithe. Many had refrained from violating the commandments. But they were proud!

In one of His parables, Jesus said, "Two men went up into the temple to pray; the one a Pharisee and the other a publican. The Pharisee stood and prayed thus with himself, 'God, I thank thee that I am not as other men are, extortioners, unjust, adulterers, or even as this publican. I fast twice in the week, I give tithes of all that I possess." And the publican, standing afar off, would not lift so much as his eyes unto heaven, but smote upon his breast, saying, 'God, be merciful to me a sinner!' I tell you, this man went down to his house justified rather than the other; for every one who exalts himself shall be abased and he that humbleth himself shall be exalted" (Luke 18:10–14).

Jesus leads us into the way everlasting. He tells us what we need to do. More than that, He explains to us that eternal life is a gift of God. He says, "Let not your hearts be troubled; believe in God, believe also in me. In my Father's house are many mansions if it were not so, I would have told you. I go to prepare a place for you. And when I go and prepare a place for you, I will come again and receive you to myself, that where I am ye may be also" (John 14:1–3).

14

The Lord's Prayer
The Meaning of the Lord's Prayer

Text: *Read Matt. 6:9–13*

Martin Luther once observed that the Lord's Prayer is the greatest of all martyrs. Sometimes the prayer is recited without thought or feeling or even faith.

The Lord's Prayer is known the world over by people in all walks of life. We like it because it expresses a depth of thought and feeling. We use it often because it is brief and familiar to us.

While the Lord's Prayer is simple in thought and expression, we find it helpful to review its meaning. Someone said the prayer is like a jewel with nine facets: an introduction, seven distinct and definite requests, and a conclusion.

The spirit in which the prayer is offered is important too, for one can approach God's glory at the beginning, wishing His name to be hallowed, asking for assistance, and praising God in His eternal glory and power.

Today we want to bring a new sensitivity to our understanding of the prayer, for our circumstances have changed: our needs may have become more personal in an impersonal, commercial, and violent age.

The Father in Heaven

The first phrase in this beautiful prayer describes God as Father. We understand that God is like a father, only in a more refined way than any earthly parent whom we may know. Yet some people may think of a father who is shiftless, lazy, irresponsible, perhaps thoughtless, or even immoral. To them it must be pointed out that fatherhood should be associated with sacrifice, dependability, high standards, discipline, and love.

Our love for the Father must be constant and strong. We can tell by our love for our fellowmen—how we treat them, how fair we are, how grateful we are—how much we respect and love the Father in heaven!

This brings us to our second major thought about the first phrase in the Lord's Prayer: We are children of God and brothers and sisters of one another. Since God is our Father, we are His children. We pray in common with others. There is a new dignity of human life portrayed in this prayer. God is our Father, our divine Friend, our Helper in time of need.

A Deep Reverence for God

Of the seven petitions in the Lord's Prayer, the first three have to do with God's desires. In the first petitions we ask that God's name be hallowed, that His kingdom come, and that His will be accomplished.

Why do people curse? We might list such reasons as an insufficient vocabulary, a desire to imitate someone who is admired, or a lack of self-control. Above all, the reason people curse is because of a lack of reverence for God. If I think a great deal of my earthly father, I won't use his name in the wrong way. Wishing God's name to be hallowed means that we want His name to have the highest respect and reverence.

The Kingdom of God

When we pray for God's kingdom to come, do we not pray for the coming of His reign, feeling that God is being forgotten, His honor disregarded, His ways ignored in a sinful world?

Earthly monarchs customarily think of kingdoms with natural boundaries such as rivers, mountains, and seas. In the Christian faith we have to deal with the human heart; the kingdom of God is inward and spiritual in nature. It has to do with righteousness and joy and peace. It is within and among us. The kingdom seems always to be in the process of growing and we find ourselves praying for its boundaries to be enlarged.

A filling station attendant once said after inspecting a flat tire, "The inner fabric is broken." The outside of the tire looked good; there was plenty of rubber left. Is this a kind of parable? Sometimes people have plenty of money, good positions, but inwardly are confused, selfish, weak. To them Jesus would not have said, "The kingdom of God is within you."

The Will of God

If it is true that "the kingdom of God is the rule of God established in the hearts and lives of men," as the *Evangelical Catechism* so beautifully states (in answer to question number 93), isn't it logical to assume that some human effort will be needed if there is to be a significant difference in the world we know? That difference comes from obedience to God's purpose and intentions. It is implied in the phrase, "Thy will be done."

We sing:

> Trust and obey,
> For there's no other way
> To be happy in Jesus
> But to trust and obey.

To do this may require a transformation by a renewal of faith if we want to prove what is the good and acceptable and perfect will of God (cf. Rom. 12:2)

Pray as if all depends on God. Apply the Word as if all depends on you!

Daily Bread

The Lord's Prayer continues with four petitions directed toward people.

An Oriental legend tells of a boy who wanted proof that God cares. A teacher took a vessel and put some earth in it. Then he said, "Watch carefully." The teacher then put a seed in the earth. In a moment there was a shoot, then a stem, leaves, branches, blossoms, and in an hour there was a tree bearing fruit. The boy responded, "Now I believe!"

The teacher said, "Just because this happened in a short time is no sign that this is any greater than what happens all the time."

God is concerned and is planting seeds everywhere but more slowly. He provides not only the earth and seed, but the sunshine and rain to nurture it. Without God it would be impossible for anything to live for even a moment.

When we pray for bread we are praying simply for the necessities of life, for the simple things we sometimes take for granted—the food on our tables, the ability to digest the food, air to breathe, sunshine and rain, and so on.

Forgiveness

When we pray for pardon we admit to our sinfulness. We can recall how we have sinned and fallen short of the glory of God. We may recognize that we have not always behaved as if we were God's children. Perhaps we have not always hallowed His name as we should. Perhaps we have not really desired that His will be done on earth as it is in heaven or that His kingdom should come in its fullness and glory. Sometimes we have not asked for daily bread in the spirit of brotherliness. When we pray for pardon in the Lord's Prayer we are asking only for something we ourselves are willing to bestow. This creates a restraining influence on ourselves and upon our prayers, because it makes us think humbly and cautiously as we approach the throne of grace.

A wife and husband were having a heated conversation about something that had come between them. The husband said to his wife, "I thought you had forgiven me." She replied, "I did, but I don't want you to forget that I have forgiven and forgotten what you have done to me." It is a devil-like thing to return evil for good, and it is a God-like thing to return good for evil. It reveals you to be a spiritual child of your heavenly Father. If we are not willing to forgive those who sin against us, "neither," said Jesus, "will your Father forgive your trespasses" (Matt. 6:15).

Temptation and Evil

Everyone, from president to pauper, is subject to temptation. The rich man may be subject to the temptations of
idleness or pride, forgetting his dependence upon God. The
businessman may be subject to the temptation of behaving
irreligiously in a world of ruthlessness and irresponsibility.
A poor man has temptations of envying others. Everyone
has temptations of envy, jealousy, greed, pride, or lust.
There are temptations that are peculiar to youth, middle
age, and even the golden years. From Bible stories we recall
that Abraham had a temptation to lie; Lot was tempted to
drink; Moses, though meek, became so angry he murdered
another. Joseph's brothers were tempted to jealousy and
repeated lies; Saul was tempted with murder and suicide.
David was tempted to commit adultery and murder. Even a
wise man like Solomon was tempted by his sensuality, pas-
sion, and desire for foreign women. There are more illustra-
tions where these come from.

An individual who had great difficulty with this part of
the Lord's Prayer thought of temptation as only an induce-
ment toward evil, whereas the primary sense in which it is
used here is a time of testing, a time of great stress and
strain, where there is a moral choice. We pray in effect,
"Lead us not into a time of testing that is too severe for us."

We continue to pray, "but deliver us from evil." We wish
to be saved from evils that lie ahead or around us, evils of
society or nature or character.

It is good that we watch and pray that we enter not into
temptations. It is good for us to know that the power of evil
is great. There is the possibility that we are morally weaker
than we imagine. We are in need of inner or spiritual

strength. When we pray we should possess the humbleness of spirit to realize that perhaps we are not as strong as we give ourselves credit.

The Kingdom, Power, and Glory

When our Lord ended this prayer, He told His disciples that they should pray "after this manner." According to footnotes in biblical translations the concluding doxology was added by early Christians.

Sometimes we hear people talk as if God is only the sum total of the goodness and love and forgiveness and cooperation of our hearts. But we have been taught that God is the Creator and Sustainer of our noblest thoughts and aspirations. God is the Creator of heaven and earth. His is the kingdom and the power and the glory.

Summary

In my imagination I would like to go to a classroom where written on the left side of the chalkboard is each phrase of the prayer and on the right side, the meaning.

"Our Father who art in heaven" refers to the Almighty Creator, the Father of our Lord Jesus Christ.

"Hallowed be thy name" means that God's name should be spoken of with deep reverence and awe.

"Thy kingdom come" involves the wish that God would rule in the hearts of all people.

"Thy will be done," means that we want God's commands and wishes to be fulfilled.

"Give us this day our daily bread" refers to our physical necessities or ordinary wants.

"Forgive us our debts" expresses our wish for the same kind of pardon we are willing to extend to other people.

"Lead us not into temptation" refers to times of testing too severe for us.

"Deliver us from evil" might read, "Help us to escape or bear the burdens and wrongs of life or triumph over them with God's help."

"For thine is the kingdom and the power, and the glory, forever"—this grand doxology means that God is over all and above all and through all, and that ultimately His world will be returned to Him in glory, even as it was His in the beginning when He created heaven and earth.

"Amen" is the word which indicates "So shall it be."

Thinking and Praying the Lord's Prayer*

(Responsively or by the officiating minister)

Pastor: Our Father who art in heaven,

People: God of life, light, and love.

Pastor: Hallowed be thy name,

People: We look up in awe and reverence.

Pastor: Thy kingdom come,

People: We look to thy world without and within.

Pastor: Thy will be done, on earth as it is in heaven.

People: We look within for strength and determination.

Pastor: Give us this day our daily bread;

People: We pray for all our basic needs.

Pastor: And forgive us our debts, as we also have forgiven our debtors;

People: We pray for pardon and peace, as we bestow pardon and peace.

Pastor: And lead us not into temptation, but deliver us from evil.

People: We pray for help in times of testing and for release from things that are wrong and wicked.

Pastor: For thine is the kingdom, and the power, and the glory forever.

People: We bow in adoration, wonder, and worship. Amen.

*Freely adapted from a prayer written by Charles Haddon Nabers, appearing in the author's *Worship Services for Church Groups,* (Philadelphia: Christian Education Press, 1962). Used by permission of the Pilgrim Press, New York.